LOVED ONE

Loved One

AN INVITATION TO FEEL
GOD'S LOVE AND TO
EXPERIENCE HIS DESIRE TO
BE YOUR GOD-SIZED HELP

Melody Bollinger

Published by Tallgrass Media
Columbia, South Carolina
books@tallgrass.media
www.tallgrass.media

Author photographs by Christine Lee Smith
Cover photograph by Phillip Berndt on unsplash.com
Cover and interior Design by Kelly Smith

Paperback ISBN: 978-0-9997626-6-0

CONTENTS

GRATITUDE

to GOD, without Whom there would be no Melody. How could I possibly express all You are to me and all You have done for me? You're showing me Your heart, which has been the cry of my heart.

to my late husband, Douglas Lyle Bollinger, whose life I shared in marriage. Because of Doug's fervent love for God and being honed by disability, I had the honor of benefitting from his inner steel-like strength. Being mostly homebound our last four years together before God took him Home opened the gateway not only for our love to grow, but more importantly, for our shared love for God to grow. It was in this time that I developed a love for writing, especially sharing the heart of God, which became so precious to us both and continues to be for me. I am grateful beyond words.

to my daughter, Christine Lee Smith, whose life is a precious gift to me from God, and who, though miles away, continues to make and shape my life more richly. I continue to be astounded at all God is doing in and through you!

to my friend, Molly Johnson. In the initial stages of this book, you encouraged me. Due to your rich and tender heart for God, I was able to share this book with you for its first touches of correction. You were gentle and I will always be grateful. Your help encouraged me not to give up when I needed reassurance!

to Dr. Terry Powell, a man sent by God at just the right time who has heart, humility and a high level of professional skills in writing and communication. God brought Doug into my life far and above what I knew to ask for in a husband. He did the same thing when He brought you into my life with regard to my writing. You came alongside to help not only with excellent communication skills, verbally and in writing, but also as a teacher/mentor to help further bring this story forward for the sake of others. Your gentle critiques, wise insight and encouragements have been and are invaluable not only for this book, but also benefit me for future work.

A WORD FROM MY HEART TO YOURS

DEAR ONE,

If you are reading this, I believe God has encouraging words to share with you. Though this story is written about a widow and a prophet, it is really about the heart of God and His extravagant care for someone in great need. I can relate, and I bet you can too. We all face times of crisis in our lives and need a lifeline of hope and help from Someone bigger than ourselves. God affectionately knows and loves you, and He invites you to know Him intimately, for to know Him is to know His heart for you.

Before you read further, I invite you to take a moment to thank God for this time with Him. Then while you read, take time to contemplate and listen for Him. Share with Him honestly from your heart. Ask the Holy Spirit to help you recognize His voice as He personally shares with you. Then let yourself listen for His gentle whispers. It's certainly not that He doesn't already know you, and all that you think and feel, but He desires for this kind of open and honest communication *with* you. This affectionate two-way communication is called communion. Communion grows deep relationship, a relationship that allows two souls to bond affectionately. My hope is that this book will help to open the eyes of your heart to further recognize God's desire for you and this kind of intimate relationship with you.

Yes, *you!*

> COMMUNION = *the sharing or exchanging of intimate thoughts and feelings.*

Try and take this in: God desires the kind of relationship with you that includes the sharing and exchanging of close-hearted thoughts and feelings. I've added places throughout this book to invite you to speak to God from your heart, but please don't let that inhibit you from communing even more with Him any time you feel inclined. At the back of the book you'll also find lined pages for notes you may wish to make. My hopeful desire is for you to let this be an experiential journey with God, one that He's personally inviting you into with Himself.

To help foster communion with God while reading this book, make an effort to create a quiet space for yourself. It will be an investment into the well-being and the advancement of your soul. I promise.

You will certainly meet God in this still place where you'll be more ready and able to hear Him. Ask the Holy Spirit to help you turn off the noise of distraction and to guard your heart and mind so that you can recognize whatever truths He wants to communicate to you. As you read, try not to let yourself rush, but let His words seep into your heart and mind. Let the Holy Spirit plant His life-affirming words deep into the soil of your spirit, where *He will foster their growth*.

Every time I have worked on this book, God has invited me into His Presence with sweet communion and encouragement. That is why I want to share it with you. I long for people to better know the heart of God, not merely from a mental point of view, but more so from an experiential, heart-related point of view. God's words are living and they are life-giving. I've no doubt that you will experience Him in a fresh way as your heart is inclined to Him.

> *"For the Word of God is alive and active. Sharper than any double-edged sword, it penetrates even to dividing soul and spirit, joints and marrow; it judges the thoughts and attitudes of the heart"* (Hebrews *4:12*).

I have prayed for you my friend, and most importantly, Jesus the Son of God and heavenly High Priest is interceding on your behalf at this very moment. As well, the Holy Spirit is also interceding God's divine desire for you *(Romans 8:34; 8:26-27)*.

With my love, and more so, God's,

A WRITING TO GIVE HOPE

The following is an interactive story about a widow, her need and God's care. Even if you are not a widow, we all find ourselves in times of need and benefit from stories that infuse our heart with encouragement and hope that nurtures growing faith.

2 Kings 4:1-7
The wife of a man from the company of prophets cried out to Elisha, "Your servant my husband is dead, and you know that he revered the LORD. But now his creditor is coming to take my two boys as his slaves." Elisha replied to her, "How can I help you? Tell me, what do you have in your house?" "Your servant has nothing there at all," she said, "except a small jar of olive oil." Elisha said, "Go around and ask all your neighbors for empty jars. Don't ask for just a few. Then go inside and shut the door behind you and your sons. Pour oil into all the jars, and as each is filled, put it to one side." She left him and shut the door behind her and her sons. They brought the jars to her and she kept pouring. When all the jars were full, she said to her son, "Bring me another one." But he replied, "there is not a jar left." Then the oil stopped flowing. She went and told the man of God, and he said, "Go, sell the oil and pay your debts. You and your sons can live on what is left."

In this true story we're not given the name of the frightened, grieving widow, so I've decided to give her a name in order to make her more personal to us as we read. While I asked the Holy Spirit what I should call her, the name Dorrah came to my mind. I don't know anyone by that name, but somehow the name Dorrah seemed fitting for an Old Testament woman. I quickly looked it up, anxious to make sure it didn't mean anything negative in case I wasn't really hearing God. Turns out, the first site where I found Dorrah's name defined its meaning as, "Gift of God." Relieved and excited, I thought, "How appropriate!" Other sites I checked revealed different definitions for the name, but since the first source I checked looks just as legitimate, I'll use the first definition found, "Gift of God."

As you walk through this dear woman's story, you will learn why this definition is fitting. She is certainly a gift from God! Her sorrow, much like King David shared in his psalms, bear encouragement and great benefit to many hurting hearts. If those who have gone before us could have only seen the outcome of God's redemptive work for the sake of others in their difficult times, they would have been astounded. If we could only understand the power of God's work in our own grievous times, our perspective would be greatly different. We would be filled with hopeful awe at the mighty work of God's hand and Plan!

Though your circumstances are likely different, my prayerful hope is that you will see yourself in some part of Dorrah's story—possibly several, and that you'll be encouraged and strengthened with comfort and hope, knowing *God makes a way where there seems to be no other way.*

THE SUPPLY OF GOD'S PROVIDENTIAL CARE RUNS DEEP.

"Forget the former things; do not dwell on the past. See, I AM doing a new thing! Now it springs up; do you not perceive it? I AM making a way in the wilderness and streams in the wasteland" (Isaiah 43:18-19).

A PRAYER FOR BEGINNING

Holy God, we come before You in the loving and powerful Name of Jesus, asking for You to still our minds and hearts as we go through Your words given us in the story of the widow, Dorrah. Help us to hear Your tender voice speak to our heart. Embed Your truths deep inside us so we may experience Your holy work and affectionate love. Thank You for desiring us and for leading us further into Your beautiful heart.

Amen.

Chapter One

FEELING LOST

*W*e are not told whether Dorrah's husband had been sick for a period of time, or if his death was sudden. Once he died, this dear widow and her sons were immediately thrown into a whole new class of people and a new lifestyle, one where their futures were unknown. Given the culture they lived in they were viewed by some with compassion and pity. Others held them with inner scorn as their needful state became evident.

This hurting mother and sons now had no means of support. Embedded in Dorrah's sorrow, among other things that we'll address later, was the loss of her perceived role in life, along with her identity. While Dorrah's husband was alive, she lived a life that was held with high regard, having the role of being a wife, and a wife of a prophet, no less. Women in that time were not considered much more valuable than a slave, except by their belonging to a man and the status that he held.

Sadly, some cultures still operate in this grievous way. Dorrah had come down from a level of recognition compared to when her husband was alive, due to his stature of being a member of the group of prophets who worked under Elisha. Now Dorrah no longer had that valued role of being a wife, much less this honored man's wife. Even though circumstances differ in our day, many of us can still relate. Whether right or wrong, we live with a degree of comfort in roles we play in life and labels we carry. When they're taken from us, it's natural to feel bewildered and lost.

I felt this when my late husband, Doug, passed from this earth. After quitting a substantial corporate job to marry and help care for him because of his physical disability, he became my honored purpose. Being his wife became my identity. When God took him Home I often found myself waking up, wondering if there was a purpose to the day God was giving me. Perhaps you've just retired, or your children have left the nest, or maybe health issues now constrain you. As a result, you may feel this same emptiness, hopelessness and fear.

Given the high-octane culture we live in, it's easy for us to mistakenly think our value is in what we do and the social status we hold. We can easily feel the grief-stricken weight of not being able to preserve a lifestyle we once knew, or a life that we believe makes us valuable. When encountering significant loss of any kind, one can feel lost being thrown into a new life where there is no longer the sense of security or the identity we have grown accustomed to. Yet, these times become an invitation to open our heart to God with a new level of honesty and to look for His intervention. TRUST HIM. He is faithful and His help will come in its perfectly appointed time!

WE MAY NOT BE ABLE TO SEE OUR FUTURE, BUT GOD DOES!

In God's hands, what appears as a dead end to us can become the gateway for a whole new level of living. When set in these constraining times, we have the opportunity to see the miraculous work of God overtake the limits of our natural world and our limited perspective. Importantly, we can experience God unlike any other kinds of times in our lives because in times like these, we are probably the most depleted of our own self-reliance. *With a more aware soul, we become deeply dependent on God and His provisionary care.* We learn that what is at first sight painful in our life can, in God's hands, be transformed into great blessing!

In Dorrah's story, you'll see how God more than provided for her, granting you hope because He has not changed *(Hebrews 13:8)*. God's same heart that loved and cared for Dorrah also loves and cares for us.

Chapter Two

THE DEBT

e don't know whether Dorrah's husband had been sick over a period of time, but if he had been, it's easy to see how easily family debt could accumulate. Or, possibly her husband's death was sudden, and Dorrah carried with her a level of shame and guilt over what may have been her family's mismanagement of money, now apparent to all who looked on. If this were the case, it's clear why she would not have felt worthy to approach Elisha to ask for help. No matter how or why her husband died, she would have had a broken and contrite heart—a state of being that pleases God no matter how well-crafted our lives appear to be *(Psalm 51:17)*.

In Dorrah's fright-filled mind, all she thought she had as potential income to cover her debts were her sons. We can see that she literally heard the voice of the enemy knocking at her door when the creditor came to her home. You likely have also known the striking grief of hearing the voice of the enemy knocking on your door. I know I have, and he's certainly no gentleman! Understandably, *fear set in as Dorrah looked at things from her limited natural view.* She was steeped in the reality that her culture's economy ran on slavery, and one's children could be taken as a high-yielding commodity when necessary, no matter the amount of anguish it caused a parent.

BUT GOD DIDN'T LOOK AT THINGS THE WAY SHE OR HER CULTURE DID. HE LOOKED IMMEASURABLY BEYOND WITH THE EXPANSE OF HIS FAR-REACHING LOVE, WISDOM AND ABILITY.

God didn't choose to use what this poor widow feared was her only viable commodity. Instead, He chose to restore her livelihood and status in the community in a way that was jaw-dropping miraculous, and in a way that she could have never dreamed of. God's work would showcase His tender love for her and her sons, and not only for their sakes, but for the watching community as well. And through the ages, *we* also get to be a part of that watching community—watching through the life-giving pages given us in Scripture.

Chapter Three

GOD'S HEART AND WISDOM

The next part in this story further reveals not only the tenderness of God's heart, but His proactive wisdom as well. Elisha, as God's representative, asks Dorrah, *"What can I do to help you?"* (v.2, NLT)

Can you imagine God asking you:

"What can I do to help you?"

He may be asking you such a question right now. If your heart is prompted, stop right here and share with Him honestly what is on your heart. He is seated so very close to you this moment, closer than you can possibly imagine.

Elisha then goes on to ask, *"Tell me, what do you have in the house?"*

May our heart be prompted to recognize when God speaks to us with the same kind of questioning, asking us:

"Tell Me, what great need do you have?"

"What do you already have that I can transform and multiply?"

Even though Elisha spoke prophetically, fulfillment of Dorrah's need wasn't to be fully realized in these first hours. God's process needed to be worked through and His appointed time was precisely set. God's help depended on levels of work not only with Dorrah, but with others who were also to be part of her story. God used Elisha, His prophet, granting him timely and forth-telling words. At this point, it's probable that Elisha was not yet privy to all God was going to do, but God was, and that is what mattered.

Maybe you're like me when in difficult circumstances and you're tempted to want to rush God's process, too. You're tired of waiting for your answer. You're weary and discouraged. If this is you, take hope! There is so much more involved in our story than we realize. God is not lethargic and uninvolved as we may sometimes think, nor is He angry with us. He brought us to this place of need in order to show-case His might and power on our behalf, and for others to see His glory manifested. Let's be patient to let God's process have its full work. God works on a God-sized platform. We will one day look back with full-blown awe at what He has accomplished far beyond our reasoning mind.

GOD'S WAITING ROOM IS NOT A PLACE OF IDLENESS.

God's waiting room is a very active room. It's often a place of internal warfare with our trust muscles being trained to hope in and rely on God's sovereign providence. It's a time of testing our resolve to let God work His Plan, while laying low our striving to take things into our own hands. It's a time of learning to rest in the sufficiency of God's provision and appointed schedule.

The enemy throws many spiraling darts at us with the intention of distracting us, but we need to call out for the help of our ever-living Friend and Counselor, the Holy Spirit. He will give us clarity to see what is true and what we're to do or not do.

Elisha asked this pain-filled woman questions, much like Jesus did with the woman at the well shared in *John 4*, and the man who was an invalid at the Pool of Bethesda in *John 5*, causing them to estimate what was true in their hearts. God's work is multifaceted. He facilitated opportunities for His loved ones to gain clarity in their heart and mind, in order to bring healing to their soul, while He also graciously worked the external answers to their need. He continues to do this with us, too.

"Nothing at all, except a flask of olive oil,' she replied" (v. 2b, NLT).

Can you see Dorrah?

She is emotionally wrung out, frightened and desperate. Sizing things up, this dear widow spoke to Elisha from the core of her being, as far as she knew to be true. She was looking at things from her natural point of view and God was going to teach her that He is not limited to that which is the natural or the supposed way of doing things. He is in fact the Creator of all things, the One Who is able to create something out from nothing and transform anything He chooses.

God honors honesty. He often pushes us to consider what we believe, not so He can learn what He already understands, but so *our* heart and mind can powerfully collide in truth. God works in the realm of truth. Our living in truth will assuredly yield great reward. Until Elisha's questioning, this dear woman believed she had nothing usable to give. Fear echoed through her being, blinding her with the searing state and probability of losing her sons. But upon having to consider what Elisha asked, she realized she did have something, though it was nothing of significance in her estimation. How could a mere flask of oil amount to anything viable, especially in the reality of such dreadful harm facing her? She couldn't yet see, *but God wasn't dependent on her seeing, only her following next steps given to her.*

Chapter Four

GOD'S POWER AND THE SEEMINGLY INSIGNIFICANT

Only her small measure of oil...

*D*orrah would learn that *what seems as nothing in human eyes becomes everything necessary and even extravagant in God's hands.* God is well able to create whatever He wants. However, He often chooses to use something or someone not recognized for worth in this world's estimation. He does this in order to showcase His brilliantly creative and transforming work while equally displaying His affectionate love.

I don't know about you, but this gives me great hope!

In God's genius, He chose to use the most seemingly insignificant commodity this impoverished widow had—her small flask of oil—in part, because its size was so very small. We see over and over again in Scripture God using the least likely people and/or resources to accomplish His purposes. He is certainly not dependent on those things we rely on or believe to be of substantial value. Instead, *God often shows forth His glorious might against the backdrop of our lack and our need* for the purpose of magnifying Himself and His glory. He also works this way for our benefit, to show Who He is in power while *revealing the tender heart He has for us behind His power.*

Chapter Five

DOING THINGS GOD'S WAY

*"And Elisha said, '**borrow as many empty jars as you can** from your friends and neighbors. Then go into your house with your sons and shut the door behind you. Pour olive oil from your flask into the jars, setting each one aside when it is filled.' So she did as she was told. Her sons kept bringing jars to her and she filled one after another. Soon every container was full to the brim! 'Bring me another jar,' she said to one of her sons. 'There aren't any more!' he told her. And then the olive oil stopped flowing"* (v.3-6, NLT).

ometimes the work of God needs to be done behind closed doors. It isn't always necessary to broadcast things God speaks to us. At times we might need to be silent because people won't understand what God has spoken to us. Their doubting reaction to what we share with them could cause us to lose focus, or possibly weaken our faith concerning the work God wants to do. I can imagine Elisha understanding the seriousness of Dorrah's need for him to help her follow through on her part without distraction, so he told her to do the work behind closed doors. This was one way God protected Dorrah and His work. In God's time, His extraordinary provision would be made evident not only to her, to her sons, and to their community, but to many more throughout the centuries who would read her story.

GOD'S WORK LIVES THROUGHOUT ETERNITY.

In other words, work that God does has purpose in this life as well as in the next. Obedience to what God clearly tells us to do may be making small steps in our estimation, but with our obedience, God's glory is announced in vast and life-giving ways when and how He determines, even to other world realms *(Ephesians 3:10, 11)*. God is in the multiplication business. What He does grows, but often in unseen places first, much like a seed that has to grow in the ground before it can spring forth and be made visible.

The pain Dorrah held was not only with regard to the creditor and her unwelcomed transition in life, but also to that of her personal loss. *The loss in Dorrah's life of losing her husband was in reality the cumulative loss of losing her companion, friend, provider, and man of God in her life.*

Dorrah was grieving this very real and great loss and feeling its weight with the fear of her unknown future. Adding to her growing fear, she still had the concern and responsibility of two sons to raise and care for. Such heaviness of heart is indescribable, unless one has traveled a similar road. I can imagine those whose spouses have left them and their children also having to face this same kind of severe strain.

What great need are you facing?

What additional responsibilities are weighing down on you because of this need?

I hope you will talk openly *with* God about it. HE IS LISTENING. He welcomes you gladly into His Presence, with a state of heart to listen and to help *(Ephesians 3:12)*.

Even in her pain, Dorrah knew to go to God through the man, Elisha. She had learned this vital dependency in the years she shared with her late husband. With divine wisdom, Elisha gave her concrete steps to take, simplifying things for her. Those in the throes of grief and despair need simple, next-step things to do. God understands these things as He thoroughly knows each of us and our need. Understandably, having created us, He knows how He made us to navigate our lives in the best possible ways.

After God took my husband Home, in grief I quickly learned that I needed life made simple. I could not handle anything lengthy, deep, or complicated.

When heavy sadness, stress or loss comes on someone, chemicals in our brain get imbalanced and can cause us to easily go into dangerous emotional overload. With God's powerful wisdom, Elisha cared for this hurting, frightened woman by giving her clear, simple steps. This is how God worked in her life and mine. He showed Himself to be compassionate and meticulous with boundless understanding, mercy and care.

Chapter Six

THE MANY FACES OF GRIEF

*E*xperiencing grief or despair doesn't always come from one's loss of a loved one. We experience loss in many ways. A writer has fittingly coined the term "Ghosts of Grief," explaining that we have many losses throughout life and they accumulate, especially if we do not mourn them.

Possibly you've experienced the loss of a job, or you've had to move. Perhaps you've experienced retirement or some other transition in life. Maybe you've gone through a divorce or have health-related issues.

MANY TIMES, WE DON'T RECOGNIZE OUR LOSSES FOR WHAT THEY REALLY ARE—SOMETHING VALUABLE THAT WE NO LONGER HAVE.

As believers, we have the ultimate Counselor in the Holy Spirit. He bids us, *"Come, and share your deepest and most honest heart with Me so I can mend what is broken."* But as long as we "fake it" and stuff our feelings inside, whether small or large, they compound, resulting in grief, depression, isolation, anxiety and despair. And equally grievous, suppressed feelings can cause a host of physical problems stemming from our internal pain.

If you recognize this is you, be open should God lead you to seek outside help, whether from a pastor, physician, professional counselor or a safe friend. God's Spirit knows you inside and out. If you will lean on Him, He will guide you in right ways because He longs for your ultimate best. *Galatians 6:2* says, *"Bear one another's burdens, and so fulfill the law of Christ" (NKJV)*. Yet no one can help us bear a burden unless we are willing to reveal it.

In short, there is no greater and healthier way to live life than to pour your heart out to God. *"Pour out your heart before Him; God is a refuge for us" (Psalm 62:8b, AMP)*.

Make time to quiet yourself enough so you can listen and hear God when He speaks. Then follow whatever way or ways He leads you. Don't let yourself fear the path. He walks before you as He leads *and He will even carry you when you can't walk.*

> *"For I AM the LORD, your God Who takes hold of your right hand and says to you, do not fear; I will help you" (Isaiah 41:13).*

God's help came in Dorrah's distress in a way that not only incorporated her participation and that of her sons, but also her neighbors (although the neighbors were not yet privy to the reason for her peculiar request in asking for jars). With God's inclusion of others, the miraculous outcome of His care became known more deeply by many more.

It's incredible to consider this:

> THE PRESSURE WASN'T ON DORRAH TO GET HER LIFE ALL FIGURED OUT.

God had it all figured out and He knew how to lead her to His good outcome, step-by-step.

God is not confined to our time,
but He works incalculably beyond
that which we physically live
and spiritually perceive.

I've found it freeing to recognize that
by the time we experience a difficulty,
God has already figured out our answer.

Chapter Seven

DON'T LIMIT GOD

*I*t's incredible to consider that Elisha told Dorrah to *"Get as many jars as you can,"* leaving open the volume of blessing she could receive. A part of Dorrah may have naturally reasoned how much oil God would multiply.

SOMETIMES OUR REASONING LIMITS WHAT GOD WOULD DO FOR US.

In this biblical story, Dorrah had the fortitude and diligence to follow the easy instructions given her. *There is something therapeutic about being given responsibility you can handle when in strained times. It lifts the mind and heart to possibility which raises hope, and hope raises faith.*

Jesus tells us,

> *"Come unto Me, all of you who are weary and carry heavy burdens, and I will give you rest. Take My yoke upon you. **Let Me teach you, because I AM humble and gentle of heart, and you will find rest for your souls"*** (Matthew 11:28-30, NLT).

I've read this Scripture countless times, but until now, I've never really taken it in. Jesus is asking us to let Him teach us. He wants to teach us so we can find rest for our souls. He wants us to experience Him *and* His rest. He knows we desperately need His rest. God is not some stoic authoritarian with a switch in His hand. He wants us to know Him, to know that He is *humble* and *gentle* of heart. We often know this about God theoretically, but does our soul *really* know this about Him? Do we recognize that His power and His desire to teach us first pours through the filter of His affectionate, humble and gentle heart? He has no need to muscle His way into our lives. But for those who desire, He puts forth the invitation of Himself *so that we can find ultimate rest.*

Jesus is that inviting.
He is that powerful.
He is that kind.

Oh, how easy it is for us to fall sway under pressurized burdens that God doesn't put on us, but instead come from the enemy through our own thoughts, or through the presumptive reasonings of others. Elisha, filled with God's Spirit, wanted Dorrah to succeed so she could experience all that God had for her. He walked beside her in the Spirit of God as her *encourager* and *helper*, much like the Holy Spirit does for us.

We need reminders of God's gentle and nurturing help because there is a prevalent mindset that works hard to deceive us into believing that God is harsh, mean, distant and even abusive. The following famous verse in Scripture speaks truth to our sometimes-waning soul that God is good and He looks out for our best good.

"For I know the plans I have for you," says the LORD. "They are for good and not for disaster, to give you a future and a hope" (Jeremiah 29:11, NLT).

Imagine what might have been going through the minds of Dorrah and her sons as they watched the flask of oil continue to pour and pour. The oil continued to flow as long as there were empty jars to fill. Remember, Elisha told her to *get as many jars as she could!* I can picture the family's great excitement experiencing such an extravagant miracle, and possibly with a tinge of regret that they didn't accumulate even more jars! In the end, I believe they were blown over with God's massive goodness to them, far more than they even knew to ask for.

Can you imagine their eagerness to run out and tell all those who helped about what great things God did for them?!

> THEIR EXCLAMATION OF GOD'S WORK DIDN'T NEED TO COME
> FROM COERCION, BUT IT CAME FROM AN EFFERVESCENT OVERFLOW
> FROM THEIR HEART BY WHAT THEY EXPERIENCED.

We might want to see this as a prized example in sharing our faith with others. I believe God wants to work in our lives so that His Spirit will freely overflow from out of us, like He did with this blessed family onto those around them. His work was quite naturally, *supernatural!*

What need has God met for you recently?

Whose faith could be encouraged if you shared how God has helped you?

Since it took faith for Dorrah to release her little bit to Elisha, I see two critical components that played out:

1. Dorrah's desperate need.
2. Her ability *to let go of her little bit* into the arms of God, revealing her hope-filled trust.

What is your little bit?

Are you willing to let it go into God's vast, loving and all-powerful arms?

The Holy Spirit, Holy God, our Friend and Helper, desires to help you. Remind yourself:

"I am not on my own to figure this all out."

Dorrah didn't have things figured out. All she did was respond. What great news this is! Find rest in the arms of Jesus, my friend. For some of us, relinquishing our grasp is more difficult than for others, so take heart if this is you. Continue to remind yourself of God's words:

> *"Let Me teach you, because I am humble and gentle of heart, and you will find rest for your souls"* (Matthew 11:29, NLT).

> *"For I know the plans I have for you," says the LORD. "They are for good and not for disaster, to give you a future and a hope"* (Jeremiah 29:11, NLT).

We find such comfort in these affirming words. That's why they were given to us. God is the God of encouragement and the epitome of wisdom and knowledge. *All good things come from Him and were made by Him.*

I, and I'm assuming many others, have found great comfort in *Matthew 11:28-30* and *Jeremiah 29:11* and have also found it beneficial to memorize these verses. In this way, the Holy Spirit fuels my soul with the truth of these promises in times of need, even when written Scripture isn't readily available.

Chapter Eight

EASING IN NEXT STEPS

"When [Dorrah] told the man of God what had happened, he said to her, 'Now sell the olive oil and pay your debts, and you and your sons can live on what is left over'" (v. 7, NLT).

ulfilling Elisha's previous instructions, Dorrah goes back to Elisha and he gave her further steps. He told her to go and sell the oil to pay her debts, then she and her sons could live on what was left. With patient guidance and support, God gently taught Dorrah to learn her part in stewardship.

Given the loss of her husband, this dear widow was now called to become her household's finance manager, and God was right there by her side to help! It may seem a little simplistic that Elisha would need to tell Dorrah to first pay her debts, but when one is in deep sorrow, rational thinking can be one of the first things to go.

I can relate to Dorrah in her pain-stricken time. Finances were never my strong suit, but they were my late husband's. He thrived on making investments and decisions. He was clear-headed and decisive

—strengths I leaned on and now greatly miss. At the same time, I've experienced God's gracious help and His ability to even carry me during this time of painful adjustment in my responsibilities. He has certainly been merciful and gentle, patient and kind.

What new responsibility, or new role, do you have due to some setback or loss in your life?

Possibly you are in such a time right now. Ask God to help you *feel* His embrace, assuring you of His nearness and divine desire to help.

We see that Dorrah had been given a substantial amount of oil to support a family of three indefinitely, at least until her sons were old enough to help support her, or until she remarried. It's possible she was not very old, since her two sons were not yet married.

TIME AND QUANTITY OF HELP NEEDED WERE NOT A PROBLEM FOR GOD IN DORRAH'S LIFE—NOR ARE THEY IN OURS!

God fully understood Dorrah's bigger story. He was the Gracious Supplier for all that she and her sons would need. *He also understands you with your need.* I believe God multiplied Dorrah's money just as He did her oil, letting it flow indefinitely for as long as was needed. For the prophet said, *"...and you and your sons can live on what is left over."* God often uses both natural and supernatural means to provide what is necessary, and in some cases, far more!

IN SHORT, THE MONEY WOULD BE THERE AS LONG AS THERE WAS NEED.

God's character, the essence of Who HE IS, is faithfulness. He is faithful to His Word. *His Word stems out from Who HE IS,* which is saying that His Word stems out of His heart. *"For out of the abundance of the heart, the mouth speaks" (Luke 6:45b, NKJV).* Looking at this story of Dorrah, we see that what comes from the heart of God is that which instills hope in us and is truly BEAUTIFUL!

Think of a time in your life when you experienced God's provision in a significant way. This kind of remembrance will bolster your faith. In the Old Testament, God had His people build altars or monuments of remembrance after He did great things for them. It's good for us to take time to look back at God's faithfulness in our lives. When we do, it encourages hope and hope builds faith. You might even consider keeping a journal or keeping a list of God's provisional care in your life to encourage and inspire you in difficult times. I encourage you to take time to thank God for His help only because I know from personal experience that life can get so busy it's easy to forget even though we don't want to. Let His past faithfulness in your life deepen your trust in Him for future needs that surface.

I started the practice of journaling words God has spoken to me and His answers to specific prayers some time ago. And I have found it to be extremely reassuring to look back on, especially in times of discouragement. When we're down, it's easy to get buried in discouraging thoughts. But when we look back and see how God has intervened in our past, hope is ignited and our faith is bolstered, aligning with truth that God really does care. The memories help us to believe God will bring us through hardship once again, and again and even again! Like Peter, when he looked at the storm, he plummeted, but when he fixed his gaze on Jesus, lifting his eyes instead onto the Truth, he found himself lifted, quite literally by the hand of God (*Matthew 14:30-31a*).

Chapter Nine

THE BIGGER GIFT

*I*n the midst of Dorrah's unnerving sorrow she showed humility and was responsive to what Elisha told her to do. When she first approached Elisha, I don't believe she anticipated the extent of blessing she was to be given. I think she was setting her hope on merely getting the creditor off her back so she wouldn't experience the horror of losing her sons to slavery. Due to her grief, it is unlikely that Dorrah was cognitively able to consider her long-term needs.

But God did!

God saw the bigger picture. He saw His story in hers, and her story in His. And with lavish grace He met more than her immediate need.

Friend, God sees beyond what you recognize as your need, and He is generous beyond what you reason.

When God doesn't answer our heartfelt prayer in a way that we have presumed or hoped, there is a greater answer waiting. We're often shortsighted, but God helps us with this also. I'd like to share an example of this from my life.

The Patience of God—His Best Awaited

After twenty-six years, my first marriage ended in divorce. About a year later, I met a man whom I fell in love with, along with his large family. I'll call him Mark. He was everything I thought I could ever want, and then some!

During the year we seriously dated, I had inklings, sometimes strongly, that this wasn't the relationship God wanted for either of us. At one point, a young man I knew to be a serious prayer warrior, and who has the spiritual gift of knowledge, believed God told him to warn me to stop the relationship. I quickly dismissed his warning, internally justifying the relationship because I was crazy about this man and wanted us to be together. I thought that together we could be "a testimony to God's work!" Mark was a powerful leader, but he also had control issues. Equally bad, when it came to women, he had a wandering heart and eye. Though Mark owned a national Christian organization, his marriage had fallen apart due to these struggles. By the time we met, his wife had remarried. But because Mark and his family lived in a small community, rumors abounded and the family was devastated.

I'm a rescuer at heart and so somehow in my own pain, I thought I could help redeem this situation. I thought I could be a part of helping to show the community, as well as Mark's family, what God could do! Even though I was not conscious of this at the time, I wanted Mark to be my answered prayer, and I wanted to be his and his family's answered prayer. Looking back, I was definitely not in an emotionally good place. With calculated wisdom and mercy, God knew I was also in need of rescuing. Logically I knew I couldn't change this strong man, but my heart couldn't understand this. Yet, God saw through the whole brokenhearted mess! Isn't it interesting how our mind can see things so differently than our heart? But God understood everything! He knew I needed protection and He was about to ensure it!

Having reservations, and based on my praying friend's warning, I wondered, "Was God really speaking to me through him?" Deep inside I knew He was, but I could also reason why my young friend had to be wrong. Even though I was vulnerable and not thinking rationally, I saw the red flags. But, I wasn't strong enough to act on what I saw to make sound decisions. So I bull-doggedly pushed forward until in God's providence, *Mark broke up with me!* He broke it off with a mere phone call on a lunch hour, of all things. I later could look back and see that keeping the call short proved to be a huge gift from God. It helped to keep my emotional hemorrhage contained, and it solidified the permanence of the breakup. Even so, the call felt like a hot serrated knife slicing through my bewildered heart.

Though I knew this to be God's work, and a very right work, I can't begin to describe the pain I experienced. I'm sure many of you know of such anguish. It's never fun to be dumped, especially by someone you feel love for and had hope for long-term plans with. What made this pain worse for me is that the severing felt more like abandonment. Fear of abandonment is something I've tried to run from all my life. In my short dating life since the divorce, I was the runner. I always made sure to leave someone before they could leave me. But this was a different story with Mark, and God was *not* using the pain for my harm. He wanted to teach me some things that were difficult, but that I needed to learn. These lessons learned would set the stage for the entrance of the man God would bring into my life, rather than continuing to experience my own destructive doing. God had to make the break clean or I would have never let the relationship go. I learned God's gentle mercy was far more than I deserved. Far more!

I don't believe I could have ended the relationship if God hadn't done it for me. Would I have asked for such a painful blow? No way! Was I *later* immensely thankful for the relationship surgery? Emphatically, YES!

Notice that I said, *later?* That's because when we've been under the Great Surgeon's knife, with His cutting away that which harms us, the process of healing is painful. But we need to let it have its needful work. After the healing comes that which we can be quite thankful for! I am reminded as I write this that God's plans for us are for our good *(Romans 8:28)*. This is true even when we don't understand and even when circumstances are sometimes so very painful. I had strongly believed Mark was God's best for me, my dream come true. Yet looking back, it would have literally become a living nightmare had we kept dating, and far worse had we married.

Are you able to look back and thank God for a prayer He did not answer the way you initially hoped He would?

If so, thank Him once again for the gracious, protective way in which He worked for you! God can never be thanked enough for His boundless care.

With my heart peeled open, and terrified of where my life was headed, I cried out to God in desperation and He heard my cry. Only two months later, God introduced me to the man I later married. Doug became the love of my life. God totally reformatted my heart with true love and a new life-giving perspective with purpose because of the life I was privileged to live with Doug. I could have never dreamed up the rewarding life that I was honored to have with him. And Doug's love and influence continue to beautifully affect my life, even though he's been in glory thirteen years as of Christmas day, 2020.

Left to my own understanding and resources, I thought I knew what I needed and wanted, but God far surpassed my understanding and met my truest heart cries, while knowing where it was that He was leading me. As Doug and I came together, we realized how God had been working behind the scenes for us to meet at just the right time in both our lives. It's really miraculous how so many things lined up in just the right time and way.

OFTEN WHILE WE WAIT, GOD IS WORKING ON THE OTHER SIDE OF OUR PRAYERS. HIS ANSWERS DEPEND ON MORE THAN WHAT IS VISIBLE.

Incredibly, I hadn't even known to ask for all that God gave me with Doug. Like Dorrah, my prayer was small, but earnest. And like Dorrah, God lavishly blessed both Doug and me in ways far beyond our natural lives. We learned that God's Plan in our lives was a divinely ordered part of His Story.

Our needs are aligned with what Joni E. Tada aptly calls, "God's wide-angled lens." Let me explain what I believe Joni means. The Holy Spirit often prompts our hearts through a need to pray God's desire into our lives, since He's acutely aware of God the Father's design for us. Because these prayers come from our need, we pray them in earnest. Remember, *"God rewards those who **earnestly** seek Him"* *(Hebrews 11:6).* Then according to God's perfect timeline, these longings and prayers are answered.

When Mark broke up with me, I somehow got through my afternoon at work, probably with tear-stained reports, but at least I got through it. When I arrived home, I melted into a puddle of tears sitting on my living room floor. From that anguish, what spilled from me was my need to know God as my loving, heavenly Father. I recall hearing my unrehearsed self say, *"I've known about You for years, but now I NEED to KNOW You as my LOVING heavenly Father!"*

Somehow I knew that this was my urgent need, and that the Holy Spirit was at work in me. He used pain to bring my true need to the surface. *Matthew 6:33* comes to mind: *"But seek first the Kingdom of God and His righteousness, and all these things will be added to you."* Without my needing to contrive it, this is what was happening in me. I was crying out for that which the Holy Spirit knew was God's desire and plan for me. And this cry would benefit me for the rest of my life, in far more ways than I knew to imagine or ask for. Like Dorrah, we don't have to have it all figured out or pray just right.

GOD IS THE DIVINE TRANSFORMER AND NOTHING IS BEYOND HIS ABILITY TO WORK FOR TRUE GOOD!

In a video celebrating her 70ᵗʰ birthday, Joni E. Tada shared that although God deeply felt the pain of her accident and paralysis *with* her, He also saw it in light of all that He was going to accomplish because of it. Joni called His work, *"God's mosaic."* That perspective, that light, reveals the miraculous and transforming work that God promises all of us who are His, no matter how tragic our situation may be. He takes that which is intended for our harm and transforms it into that which breathes life into us and out from us. Joni and Doug were able to come to a place of thanking God *for* their accidents because of how God used them *because* of those accidents.

For many of us, some of the most trying times are those when we are in transition. I was in transition after the breakup with Mark and before meeting Doug. I had no clue where my life was heading, and honestly, it was scary. There were times my stomach churned with anxiety, but I continued to cry out to God.

During transitional times we may sense God's direction, but the *not there yet* is hard. Or, perhaps we have no clue where God is taking us. Either way, we feel unsettled, as if suspended. Yet God can't lose us or His plan, even when we feel as lost and as terrified as I did.

My life with Doug—except for my daughter's birth and her growing years—held the most solidly purposed years of my life. *I felt heavenly anchored.* In that difficult, suspended time before I met Doug, I had no clue I would be gifted such a fine man who was deeply in love with God. As amazing as our knowing times are, we don't get to live in them all the time. If we did, we'd stop growing and we wouldn't value the joys given us in contrast to the uncertain times. God actually used my heartbreak and painful transition to usher me into His next blessing in my life.

Can you think of a time when you felt you were exactly where you were supposed to be?

I can imagine you cherish those memories. I know I do! Their remembrances help to hearten us through the other times of our lives when we have to walk where we don't see our way clearly.

It's rewarding for me to look back with growing understanding, recognizing that those brief years with Doug continue to richly benefit my life. Doug's life poured into mine generous gifts on so many levels. Left to my own devices, I would have settled for so little—a life void of the best journey God had for me. God, with gracious, strategic wisdom, knew how to bring me back around to what He had waiting for me when I let go of my tenacious, short-sighted grip. Though the process to arrive there was painful, the rewards have far exceeded the season of anguish.

What I realized in my marriage with Doug was that the lifestyle God afforded us was the precise environment I needed to answer my heart cry—to know God personally, not just know about Him. It provided circumstances that enabled intimacy to grow with God, which I had longed for since that painful time of breaking up with Mark. In this new season, I lived in communion with God in a way that fostered my ability to *feel* His love as my caring heavenly Father. This would have never happened with the constraints I would have lived with had I married Mark. But with Doug's passionate love for God and our quieted lifestyle—being confined at home so much and with great need—we both experienced the rich Presence of God, as if Heaven came down. Our natural lives were often painful, yet at the same time, our spirits soared. It's a peculiar dichotomy, but nonetheless, real.

Can you recall a time that was scary or bitterly painful, and at the same time, you felt enveloped by God?

God's ways are brilliantly creative, and His narrative in both Doug's life and mine was quite a miraculous one. One that God worked entirely out of the box for the sake of redeeming both of our broken lives. In addition to all this, and much I've not shared, we were both given the privilege to recognize that our marriage truly did originate in Heaven. Only God could do such imaginative, multifaceted work!

Ultimately, God met my need in ways that exceeded my desires and expectations. Like He did with Dorrah, God lavished His grace and provision on me. And He desires to do this same work in your life! It will look different, but it will be rich with God's Divine Creativity designed personally for you.

IF YOU GAZE ON HIM WHO PROVIDES ALL GOOD THINGS, YOU
WILL LEARN HIS GAZE IS ALREADY SET ON YOU.

Doug's mom, Virginia, took this picture of us while visiting us our first year together, 2003. It wasn't a planned picture or I would have at least had shoes on. (Smile.) On the other hand, Doug was always impeccably dressed.

Chapter Ten

MAKING IT PERSONAL

Are you facing great need with no might, no clarity and possibly teetering with lost hope?

Are you one who knows your dire need for saving grace right here and now, in this place in your life?

---

*J*esus, Son of God, LORD and Friend, longs to be gracious to you. Talk to Him. Open your heart with honesty to *"Him Who sticks closer than a brother"* (Proverbs 18:24b), to Him Who is faithful, and Whose story you've been invited to be a part.

REMEMBER: Dorrah didn't have much in her hand, but God multiplied it.

Might Jesus be asking you right now,

"Beloved, what is in your hand?"

"What is in your life that I have given you that I can multiply?"

Perhaps God's Spirit is saying to you, "Come to Me with courage, like the widow Dorrah, asking with a humble heart. I will supply hope which will help your faith to grow, for in My hands, all is possible." *(See Jesus' promise in Mark 9:23.)*

Dear one, if you don't know what you have to give, ask the Holy Spirit to help you to recognize what you hold. Take time to prayerfully look into your heart and consider what He reveals to you, and consider that not everything you or any of us hold is visible or tangible. Let God help you see what He sees, to help you to look beyond that which is naturally limited. Be open to the whispers the Holy Spirit speaks to your heart.

God's work wasn't dependent on Dorrah being eloquent in her request. Basically, she said, "HELP! I'm in trouble!! Here's what I fear!" She was honest and her request was urgent. Dorrah's earnest plea was much like that which King David exemplified for us in his psalms. I've included one below. Notice the simplicity of his prayer to God, along with his humility and childlike honesty. Certainly not childish, but childlike *(also see a childlike attitude called for in Matthew 18:3).*

> *"Hear me, LORD, and answer me, for I am poor and needy. Guard my life, for I am faithful to You; save Your servant who trusts in You. You are my God; have mercy on me, LORD, for I call to You all day long. Bring joy to Your servant, LORD, for I put my trust in You. You, LORD, are forgiving and good, abounding in love to all who call to You. Hear my prayer, LORD; listen to my cry for mercy. When I am in distress, I call to You, because You answer me" (Psalm 86:1-7).*

God afforded us in Scripture the treasure of seeing David's heart in his psalms in order to help us learn what it is that He values: a true (open, honest), humble, and contrite heart that looks to, longs for, and seeks Him. David as well as Dorrah epitomized the attitude called for in *Isaiah 66:2.*

"To this one I will look (graciously), to him who is humble and contrite of spirit, and who (reverently) trembles at My word and honors My commands" (AMP).

WON'T YOU JOIN ME IN PRAYER?

You are my Holy Father, Gracious Father, Supplier of all my need. Thank You for Jesus, Your Son, and for desiring me to be part of Your life. I cannot fathom the largeness of Who You are, but You help me by the Holy Spirit to feel the assurance of Your Presence just when I need to.

(Now dear one, pour out your heart to God in whatever way that is natural for you. He's so close to you, already having prepared this time for you to open up. Then listen and let Him show you His own heart.)

Chapter Eleven

AN INVITATION

For Those Who Don't Yet Know Jesus Christ Personally

*S*ome of you reading this book may not yet know Jesus Christ as your Savior, LORD and Friend. If you want a growing and thriving relationship with Him, and also to secure eternal life in Heaven, I invite you to talk with Him. He created you. He can hear you. He's the God Who listens to sincere, honest and humble hearts.

Ask Him to make Himself real to you. He will, and in a way that is personal because *you* are personal to Him. Ask Him to forgive your sins (those things you've done wrong). Scripture tells us that *we all* have sinned and come short of God's best *(Romans 3:23a)*. Yet that doesn't have to be the end of your story. God has paved the way for your forgiveness and mine, so that we can enter into a relationship with Him by the blood-bought sacrifice of Jesus Christ, His Son, on our behalf.

> *"For God so loved the world that He gave His one and only Son, that whoever believes in Him shall not perish but have eternal life" (John 3:16).*

"You will seek Me and find Me when you search for Me with all your heart" (Jeremiah 29:13).

Tell God that you believe Jesus' death on the cross paid the penalty for those things you've done wrong, and that you believe He rose from the dead. Let God know you love Him and want His enablement to live for Him. Then ask Him to help you know what to do next. He's God. He knows how to help you. It's what He desires!

I'd like to encourage you to get a Bible and ask God to help you understand it. If you can't afford one, many churches will be happy to give you one if you ask. There are also many websites that host the Bible free online. A few that I value are: biblegateway.com, blueletterbible.org and biblehub.com. For those of you who are more tech savvy, there are also apps you can download onto your phone. The Bible is God's Word to us to help us grow in knowledge of Him so we can know Him. It also helps to facilitate a communing relationship with Him.

There are many different versions of the Bible with some easier to read than others. I personally don't recommend starting with a King James Version (KJV). It's more archaic in language. But whether you start with this version or any other, God's Word is living. The New Living Bible (TLB) was the first Bible I used. It was an easy, relatable read. Later, I found the Amplified Bible (AMP) to be more detailed, helping me to better understand what the verses were telling me. Now I use multiple versions with some that have study notes and commentary that is helpful. Whatever version you choose, the Holy Spirit will certainly help you to grow in your understanding, while leading you into a close, communing relationship with God as you look to and desire Him.

There is no formula to the order you should read the Bible, but I personally think starting in the Gospel of John in the New Testament is beneficial. It's one of the four books in the New Testament where Jesus' words as both God and man are recorded in an especially personal way, with Jesus speaking to His disciples while He was on earth in physical form. What Jesus said to His disciples at that time also applies to us living now! In many Bibles, Jesus' words are written in red ink to make them easier to distinguish. His words are recorded in four of the books of the New Testament: Matthew, Mark, Luke and John. You can find where their pages are in the front of the Bible, in the Table of Contents or simply, Contents section. (*Incidentally, a disciple is one who follows Jesus, one who is in relationship with Him.*)

There is a beautiful prayer from Jesus for His loved ones (including us!) in *John 17* that I find extremely comforting. I especially love verse twenty-four where Jesus is telling God the Father, *"Father, I want those You have given Me to be with Me where I am, and to see My glory, the glory You have given Me because You loved Me before the creation of the world"* (*John 17:24*).

Is this not incredible?! Jesus deeply wants those of us who love Him to be with Him forever, to see the magnificence of His glory for eternity! Our being in relationship with Jesus means we get to be a part of His life and all that God the Father has given Him. Just like when we love someone, we want them to really know us and we want to share our lives with them and all that we have. It's the same way with God, but so much more!

Additionally, I believe you will find the book of Psalms in the Old Testament (found approximately in the center of the Bible) encouraging and comforting. A lot of the psalms were written by the powerful King David, who had a tender heart for God. You will also see God's tender heart for him, which is the same tender heart He has for us. The psalms are written in prayer form, including both praises and thanksgiving to God. You'll see King David's and the other authors' honest and humble crying out to God for His timely help as they faced many severe troubles. King David knew great heartache, but he also knew the compassionate love of God to minister comfort, and to grant him apt and supernatural help—always on time!

God wants a personal journey with you because *you* are His uniquely personal creation. Talk to Him naturally. He's a listener of the heart and wants an authentic and genuine relationship with you, not a contrived or formulated one. He's a personal and relational God, the only TRUE GOD, and the only God Who has the power and desire to give you a new life right now *and* throughout eternity!

For those embarking on this new journey with Jesus, I pray He will open your eyes and heart to know the richness of His love and Presence, and may He guard your steps. May He lead you into truth, for He is TRUTH, and all that is true comes from Him.

I am praying for you, dear one. God knows who you are and He sends His love to you with this unfathomable invitation, saying, *"Come to Me and learn of Me."* He longs to share His heart with you, and have you share yours with Him.

Lastly, I pray that God will help you find a church that is right for you in this new season of your life so that you can be knitted into a family with other believers to worship together, have friendships and be taught God's Word.

I'm concluding with *Psalm 139:1-18,* written by King David. I believe that it will help you to more fully realize how personally you've been created and how deeply and affectionately loved you are by God.

If you already have a personal relationship with the LORD, read *Psalm 139,* taking time to identify the words and phrases that encourage you or that declare something important to you about God. What you further learn about Him will instill in you more faith, which will help prompt you to take your personal needs and cares to Him. Like Dorrah, you'll discover how lavish God's love and generosity are.

Closing with my love, and even more so, God's love,

PSALM 139:1-18

You have searched me, LORD,
and You know me.
You know when I sit and when I rise;
You perceive my thoughts from afar.
You discern my going out
and my lying down;

You are familiar with all my ways.
Before a word is on my tongue,
You, LORD, know it completely.
You hem me in behind and before,
and You lay Your hand upon me.
Such knowledge is too wonderful for me,
too lofty for me to attain.

Where can I go from Your Spirit?
Where can I flee from Your presence?
If I go up to the heavens, You are there;
if I make my bed in the depth, You are there.

If I rise on the wings of dawn,
if I settle on the far side of the sea,
even there Your hand will guide me,
Your right hand will hold me fast.

If I say, "Surely the darkness will hide me
and the light become night around me,"
even the darkness is as light to You.

For You created my inmost being,
You knit me together in my mother's womb.
I praise You because
I am fearfully
and wonderfully made;
Your works are wonderful,
I know that full well.

My frame was not hidden from You
when I was made in the secret place,
when I was woven together
in the depths of the earth.
Your eyes saw my unformed body;
all the days ordained for me
were written in Your book
before one of them came to be.

How precious to me
are Your thoughts, God!
How vast is the sum of them!
Were I to count them,
they would outnumber the grains of sand—
when I awake, I am still with You.

ABOUT THE AUTHOR

*M*elody Bollinger is a seeker of God's heart. Her passion is to express in writing what she has experienced so that others might also experience the joy and richness of intimacy *with* God. Even though Melody spent most of her life loving God, in reality, the depth of her relationship with Him was merely knowing *about* Him. All that changed when she hit what she remembers as a virtual breaking point in her life. In a greatly painful time, she cried out in earnest to *know* God and not just *about* Him. He heard that cry and her life took a drastic turn, changing her heart and her life in ways she never imagined.

Since that initially painful time, an exceptional journey has ensued by the loving invitation of God Who longs to be known by all His loved ones. She is learning that His desire is for relationship *with* His beloveds. One that is not religiously cliché, but one that resides with authenticity and desire.

Melody spends most of her time reading, studying and writing. Even though she has written five books, this is the first one published. She also enjoys writing short inspirational devotionals that she shares on her Facebook Page. All her writing is centered on themes of encouragement and hope under the canopy of God's tenderness. Her passionate pursuit of God's affectionate heart has led her to understand that when able to experience His heart, one is drawn more deeply in love with Him.

Road trips and eating out are some of Melody's favorite things to do. She enjoys country roads best and her culinary tastes range anywhere from old time diners to fine dining. She also enjoys movies, with true stories and documentaries being among her favorites.

Made in the USA
Las Vegas, NV
04 March 2021